GRAPHIC HISTORIES
THE BATTLE OF GETTYSBURG

STORY:
KERRI O'HERN AND DALE ANDERSON

ILLUSTRATIONS:
D. MCHARGUE

WORLD ALMANAC® LIBRARY

B

Y 1863, THE CIVIL WAR HAD BEEN GOING ON FOR TWO YEARS. THAT YEAR, ONE BATTLE BECAME THE BLOODIEST OF THE ENTIRE CIVIL WAR. THE ARMIES OF THE NORTH AND THE SOUTH FOUGHT IN THE SMALL TOWN OF GETTYSBURG, PENNSYLVANIA. THIS VIOLENT BATTLE RAGED ON FOR THREE DAYS. OVER 50,000 SOLDIERS WERE EITHER INJURED OR KILLED. THE SOUTH'S LOSSES WERE ESPECIALLY HIGH—HIGH ENOUGH TO AFFECT THE OUTCOME OF THE CIVIL WAR.

THE CIVIL WAR, WHICH BEGAN IN 1861 AND ENDED IN 1865, WAS FOUGHT OVER TWO MAIN ISSUES. ONE WAS SLAVERY. THE OTHER WAS KEEPING THE UNITED STATES (OR THE UNION, AS IT ALSO CAME TO BE CALLED) UNITED AS A SINGLE NATION.

IN 1860, JUST MONTHS BEFORE THE CIVIL WAR BEGAN, ABRAHAM LINCOLN WAS ELECTED PRESIDENT OF THE UNITED STATES. SOUTHERNERS FEARED LINCOLN WOULD MAKE SLAVERY ILLEGAL. SLAVES PICKED COTTON FOR SOUTHERN PLANTATION OWNERS. COTTON MADE A LOT OF MONEY FOR THE SOUTH.

PEOPLE LIVING IN THE NORTH DID NOT APPROVE OF SLAVERY. THEY ALSO WANTED TO KEEP THE UNION WHOLE.

APRIL 12, 1861 . . .

SOUTHERNERS WANTED TO TAKE CONTROL OF FORT SUMTER, A U.S. MILITARY POST OFF THE COAST OF SOUTH CAROLINA. THIS FORT WAS NOW LOCATED IN A CONFEDERATE STATE. FORCES FROM SOUTH CAROLINA WANTED TO PUT IT IN SOUTHERN HANDS. WHEN THE UNION COMMANDER REFUSED TO GIVE IT UP . . .

FIRE!

. . . CONFEDERATE CANNONS OPENED FIRE! THE FIRST SHOTS BETWEEN THE NORTH AND THE SOUTH BLASTED ONTO FORT SUMTER.

CANNON BALLS POUNDED THE FORT FOR TWO DAYS.

UNION SOLDIERS FOUGHT BRAVELY. . .

RETURN FIRE!

. . . BUT THEY COULD HOLD OUT NO LONGER.

THE CONFEDERATES TOOK CONTROL OF THE FORT, AND . . .

. . . THE CIVIL WAR HAD BEGUN.

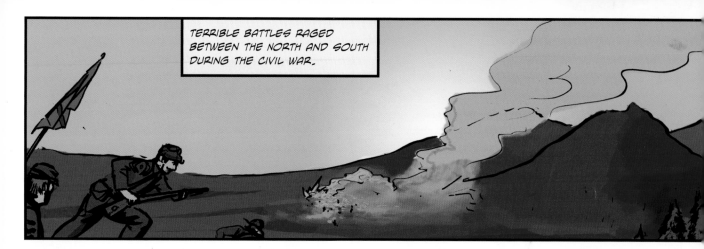

TERRIBLE BATTLES RAGED BETWEEN THE NORTH AND SOUTH DURING THE CIVIL WAR.

GUNS AND CANNONS BLASTED.

MEN CHARGED UP HILLS AND ACROSS FIELDS. AND MANY MEN DIED.

CHARGE!

BAM BOOM POP

BY THE SPRING OF 1863, THE UNION CONTROLLED MOST OF THE MISSISSIPPI RIVER. THIS RIVER WAS A VERY VALUABLE WATERWAY.

EVEN AFTER YEARS OF FIGHTING, THE UNION STILL HAD LOTS OF TROOPS AND SUPPLIES.

THE CONFEDERATES, ON THE OTHER HAND, HAD LOST A LOT OF MEN. THEY ALSO HAD FEW SUPPLIES.

ONE OF THE REASONS WHY THE SOUTH KEPT FIGHTING WAS DUE TO ITS BRILLIANT LEADER—GENERAL ROBERT E. LEE. HE HAD EXCELLENT BATTLE PLANS, AND HIS TROOPS FOLLOWED HIS ORDERS!

IN JANUARY 1863, PRESIDENT LINCOLN ISSUED THE EMANCIPATION PROCLAMATION. THIS DOCUMENT FREED SLAVES IN THE SOUTH—BUT ONLY IF THE NORTH WON THE WAR! SOUTHERNERS WERE FURIOUS—ESPECIALLY THE RICH PLANTATION OWNERS!

WHO DOES ABE LINCOLN THINK HE IS? HE HAS NO POWER HERE!

HAVE YOU HEARD THE NEWS?

THE SLAVES COULD BARELY BELIEVE THE GREAT NEWS!

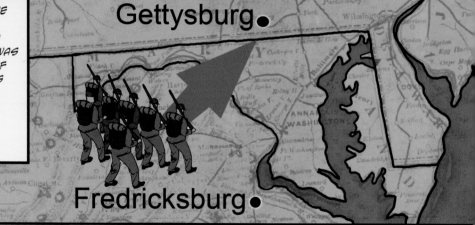

NOW, MORE THAN EVER BEFORE, THE CIVIL WAR BECAME A FIGHT ABOUT SLAVERY. LEE KNEW HE HAD TO DO SOMETHING TO END THIS WAR. IT WAS TIME TO MOVE THE BATTLES OFF OF SOUTHERN LANDS. HE MARCHED HIS TROOPS TOWARD PENNSYLVANIA IN EARLY JUNE, 1863. LEE FIRST MOVED HIS TROOPS WEST FROM FREDERICKSBURG, VIRGINIA, THEN TURNED HIS ARMY NORTH.

Gettysburg

Fredricksburg

BY JULY 1, 1863, BOTH SIDES HAD HUGE ARMIES IN AND AROUND GETTYSBURG. GENERAL LEE'S ARMY HAD ABOUT 75,100 CONFEDERATE SOLDIERS. GENERAL MEADE'S ARMY HAD ABOUT 83,300 UNION SOLDIERS.

THE BATTLE . . .

MORE SOLDIERS ARRIVED FOR BOTH SIDES.

GENERAL LEE CAME TO TAKE CHARGE AND LIFT THE CONFEDERATE SOLDIERS' SPIRITS.

AS THE FIGHTING CONTINUED . . .

ARGGH!

. . . DEAD SOLDIERS LAY EVERYWHERE.

THE UNION ARMY RETREATED TO HIGH GROUND.

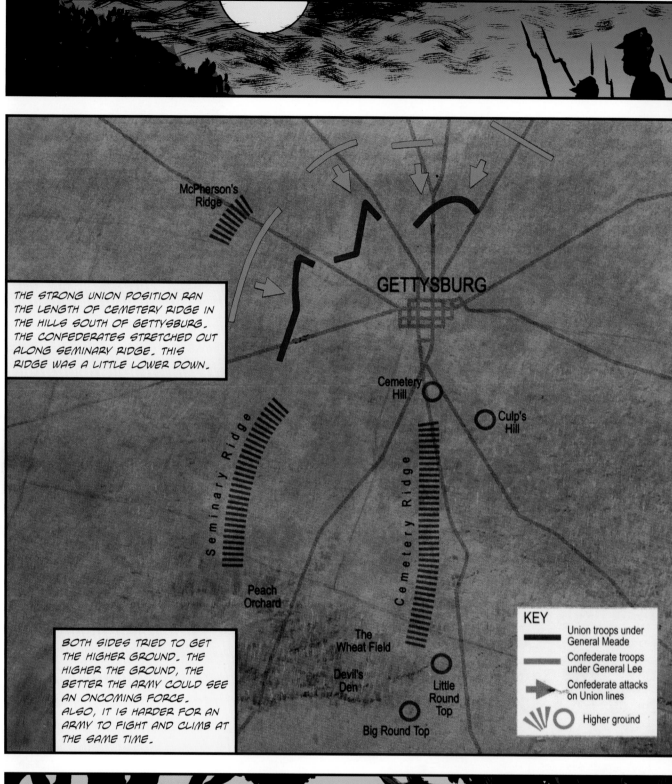

McPherson's Ridge

GETTYSBURG

THE STRONG UNION POSITION RAN
THE LENGTH OF CEMETERY RIDGE IN
THE HILLS SOUTH OF GETTYSBURG.
THE CONFEDERATES STRETCHED OUT
ALONG SEMINARY RIDGE. THIS
RIDGE WAS A LITTLE LOWER DOWN.

Cemetery Hill

Culp's Hill

Seminary Ridge

Cemetery Ridge

Peach Orchard

The Wheat Field

Devil's Den

Little Round Top

Big Round Top

BOTH SIDES TRIED TO GET
THE HIGHER GROUND. THE
HIGHER THE GROUND, THE
BETTER THE ARMY COULD SEE
AN ONCOMING FORCE.
ALSO, IT IS HARDER FOR AN
ARMY TO FIGHT AND CLIMB AT
THE SAME TIME.

KEY

Union troops under General Meade

Confederate troops under General Lee

Confederate attacks on Union lines

Higher ground

DAY TWO . . .

LEE ORDERED HIS MEN TO TAKE THE HILLS CALLED ROUND TOPS, SOUTH OF CEMETERY RIDGE. HIS PLAN? TO CONQUER THE UNION FORCES.

SUDDENLY, A UNION GENERAL SAW THE CONFEDERATES COMING! HE RACED DOWN THE HILL TO DEFEND THE UNION'S POSITION.

BOOM

KNOWING THEY WOULD DIE OR BE WOUNDED, UNION SOLDIERS STILL DEFENDED THIS POSITION. AFTER A BRUTAL FIGHT, THE CONFEDERATES ENDED THEIR ATTACK.

DAY TWO, CONTINUED . . .

A VIOLENT FIGHT BROKE OUT IN THE PEACH ORCHARD. THE CONFEDERATES CHARGED THROUGH THE ORCHARD. THEY STOPPED RIGHT IN FRONT OF THE UNION DEFENDERS. THE SOLDIERS FOUGHT FACE TO FACE. HALF OF THE UNION MEN DIED WITHIN MINUTES.

THIS TIME, THE UNION ARMY RETREATED . . .

... BUT THE NUMBERS OF WOUNDED AND DEAD ON BOTH SIDES WERE HUGE.

DOCTORS AND NURSES DID THE BEST THEY COULD TO HELP THE WOUNDED. THEY COULD BARELY KEEP THE WOUNDS CLEAN OF INFECTIONS. THE LEAD BALLS USED AS BULLETS SHATTERED BONES. MANY INJURED SOLDIERS LOST THEIR ARMS OR LEGS. THOUSANDS DIED LATER FROM INFECTED WOUNDS OR BLOOD LOSS.

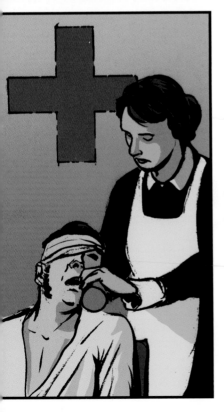

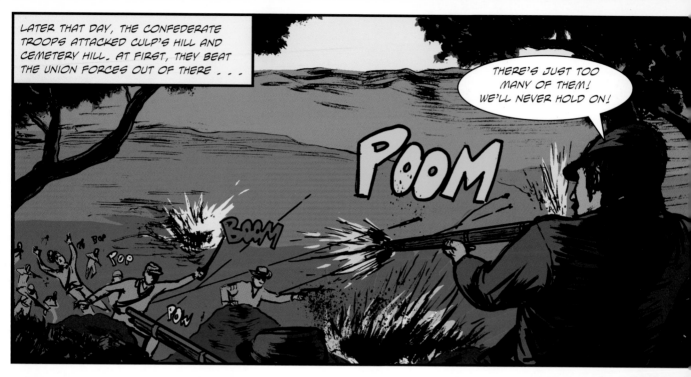

LATER THAT DAY, THE CONFEDERATE TROOPS ATTACKED CULP'S HILL AND CEMETERY HILL. AT FIRST, THEY BEAT THE UNION FORCES OUT OF THERE . . .

THERE'S JUST TOO MANY OF THEM! WE'LL NEVER HOLD ON!

POOM

BOOM

POP

POP

. . . BUT THE RETREATING UNION SOLDIERS GATHERED THEIR FORCES AND CHARGED BACK.

WHERE'D ALL THEM NORTHERN BOYS COME FROM? RETREAT!

THE CONFEDERATES HAD TO PULL BACK TO THEIR TRENCHES ON THE HILL.

AS THE SUN BEGAN TO SET ON DAY TWO . . .

THE SKY TURNED DARK, AND MORE UNION TROOPS ARRIVED. THE CONFEDERATE SOLDIERS COULD NOT SEE THE EXTRA UNION SOLDIERS COMING.

WHAT'S THAT OVER THERE?

SUDDENLY, THE UNION SOLDIERS WERE RIGHT IN FRONT OF THEM.

BY THE END OF THE DAY, THE CONFEDERATES HAD TAKEN THE PEACH ORCHARD AND THE WHEAT FIELD. THE UNION FORCES HAD KEPT THEIR HIGH GROUND ON CEMETERY RIDGE AND GAINED THE ROUND TOPS.

BENEATH THE SMOKE AND CHAOS OF THE BATTLEFIELD, THE CONFEDERATE ARMY HAD SUFFERED TERRIBLE LOSSES—PICKETT HAD LOST ABOUT TWO-THIRDS OF HIS MEN.

HOLD YOUR FIRE, BOYS. THEY'RE RETREATING. IT'S OVER!

SOLDIERS ON BOTH SIDES KNEW THIS FIGHT WAS OVER—AND THE CONFEDERATES HAD LOST.

PICKETT'S CHARGE WAS OVER . . .

. . . AND SO, GENERAL LEE KNEW, WAS THE BATTLE OF GETTYSBURG.

HELP . . .

GENERAL LEE WATCHED WHAT WAS LEFT OF HIS ARMY RETURN FROM THEIR DOOMED ATTACK.

IT'S ALL MY FAULT. IT IS I WHO HAVE LOST THIS FIGHT.

BY JULY 5, 1863—TWO DAYS AFTER THE BATTLE THE CONFEDERATES HAD LEFT GETTYSBURG. OVERALL, THE CONFEDERATE ARMY HAD 28,000 DEAD OR WOUNDED, THE UNION HAD ABOUT 23,000. THE CIVIL WAR DID NOT LAST MUCH LONGER AFTER GETTYSBURG.

A CEMETERY WAS CREATED AT GETTYSBURG BY NORTHERN GOVERNORS.

FOURSCORE AND SEVEN YEARS AGO OUR FOREFATHERS BROUGHT FORTH ON THIS CONTINENT, A NEW NATION, CONCEIVED IN LIBERTY, AND DEDICATED TO THE PROPOSITION THAT ALL MEN ARE CREATED EQUAL.

ON NOVEMBER 19, 1863, PRESIDENT LINCOLN GAVE A SPEECH TO HONOR THE DEAD AT THIS BATTLEGROUND. DURING HIS SPEECH, KNOWN AS THE GETTYSBURG ADDRESS, HE SPOKE ABOUT HIS HOPE THAT THE NORTH AND SOUTH WOULD UNITE. LINCOLN REMINDED LISTENERS WHY THE UNITED STATES WAS GREAT. THE COUNTRY HAD BEEN FOUNDED IN 1776 WITH THE BELIEF THAT "ALL MEN ARE CREATED EQUAL." LINCOLN HOPED TO SEE AMERICANS LIVE TOGETHER AS ONE NATION AGAIN. THE U.S. CIVIL WAR FINALLY ENDED IN 1865. MORE AMERICANS DIED IN THE CIVIL WAR THAN IN ANY OTHER WAR IN U.S. HISTORY. AS LINCOLN SAID, THEY DIED "SO THAT THIS NATION . . . SHALL HAVE A NEW BIRTH OF FREEDOM."

MORE BOOKS TO READ

Battle of Gettysburg. Battles That Changed the World (series). Earle Rice
   (Chelsea House Publishers)

The Battle of Gettysburg. Cornerstones of Freedom (series). Dan Elish (Children's Press)

The Battle of Gettysburg. Landmark Events in American History (series). Jane Riehecky
   (World Almanac Library)

Civil War Ghosts. Daniel Cohen (Scholastic)

Rosa Parks: My Story. Rosa Parks (Penguin Putnam Books for Young Readers)

A Day That Changed America: Gettysburg. A Day That Changed America (series).
   Shelley Tanaka (Hyperion Books for Children)

If You Lived When There Was Slavery in America. Anne Kamma (Scholastic)

WEB SITES

The Battle of Gettysburg
www.americancivilwar.com/kids_zone/gettysburg_battle.html

Civil War Chronicles
www.discovery.com/stories/history/civilwar/gettysburg/gettysburg.html

The Civil War for Kids
www2.lhric.org/pocantico/civilwar/cwar.htm

Gettysburg National Military Park Kidzpage
www.nps.gov/gett/gettkidz/kidzindex.htm

A War to End Slavery
www.pbs.org/wnet/historyofus/web06/

Please visit our web site at: www.worldalmanaclibrary.com
For a free color catalog describing World Almanac® Library's list
of high-quality books and multimedia programs,
call 1-800-848-2928 (USA) or 1-800-387-3178 (Canada).
World Almanac® Library's fax: (414) 332-3567.

Library of Congress Cataloging-in-Publication Data

O'Hern, Kerri.
    The battle of Gettysburg / Kerri O'Hern and Dale Anderson.
       p. cm. — (Graphic histories)
    Includes bibliographical references.
    ISBN 0-8368-6204-X (lib. bdg.)
    ISBN 0-8368-6256-2 (softcover)
    1. Gettysburg, Battle of, Gettysburg, Pa., 1863—Juvenile literature.
 I. Anderson, Dale, 1953- II. Title. III. Series.
 E475.53.O38 2006
 973.7'349—dc22   2005027873

First published in 2006 by
World Almanac® Library
A Member of the WRC Media Family of Companies
330 West Olive Street, Suite 100
Milwaukee, WI 53212 USA

Copyright © 2006 by World Almanac® Library.

Produced by Design Press, a division of the
Savannah College of Art and Design
Design: Janice Shay and Maria Angela Rojas
Editing: Kerri O'Hern
Illustration: D. McHargue
World Almanac® Library editorial direction: Mark Sachner
    and Valerie J. Weber
World Almanac® Library art direction: Tammy West

Printed in the United States of America

1 2 3 4 5 6 7 8 9 10 09 08 07 06